I0815523

Music Superstars
BTS
TORQUE
BY SUZANE NGUYEN
BELLWETHER MEDIA · MINNEAPOLIS, MN

Torque brims with excitement perfect for thrill-seekers of all kinds. Discover daring survival skills, explore uncharted worlds, and marvel at mighty engines and extreme sports. In *Torque* books, anything can happen. Are you ready?

This edition first published in 2025 by Bellwether Media, Inc.

No part of this publication may be reproduced in whole or in part without written permission of the publisher. For information regarding permission, write to Bellwether Media, Inc., Attention: Permissions Department, 6012 Blue Circle Drive, Minnetonka, MN 55343.

Library of Congress Cataloging-in-Publication Data

Names: Nguyen, Suzane, author.
Title: BTS / by Suzane Nguyen.
Description: Minneapolis, MN : Bellwether Media, 2025. | Series: Music superstars | Includes bibliographical references and index. | Audience: Ages 7-12 | Audience: Grades 4-6 | Summary: "Engaging images accompany information about BTS. The combination of high-interest subject matter and light text is intended for students in grades 3 through 7"– Provided by publisher.
Identifiers: LCCN 2024047016 (print) | LCCN 2024047017 (ebook) | ISBN 9798893042634 (library binding) | ISBN 9798893043600 (ebook)
Subjects: LCSH: BTS (Musical group)–Juvenile literature. | Singers–Korea (South)–Biography–Juvenile literature. | Rock musicians–Korea (South)–Biography–Juvenile literature. | Boy bands–Korea (South)–Juvenile literature. | LCGFT: Biographies.
Classification: LCC ML3930.B89 N58 2025 (print) | LCC ML3930.B89 (ebook) | DDC 781.630922 [B]–dc23/eng/20241008
LC record available at https://lccn.loc.gov/2024047016
LC ebook record available at https://lccn.loc.gov/2024047017

Text copyright © 2025 by Bellwether Media, Inc. TORQUE and associated logos are trademarks and/or registered trademarks of Bellwether Media, Inc.

Editor: Rachael Barnes   Designer: Josh Brink

Printed in the United States of America, North Mankato, MN.

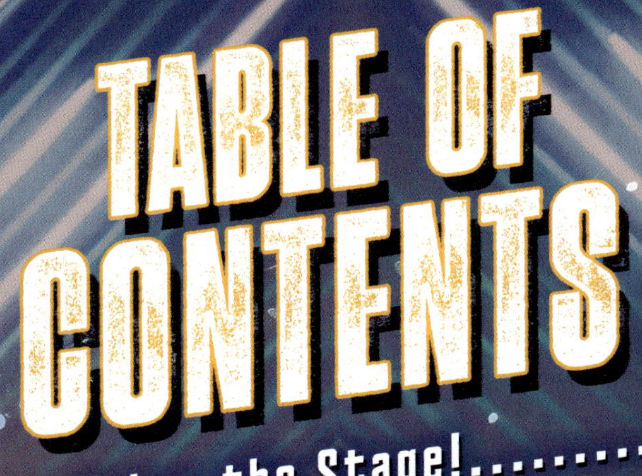
TABLE OF
CONTENTS

K-POP TAKES THE STAGE!

It is the 2022 **Grammy Awards**. One by one, BTS members make their way to the stage from the crowd. The boy band begins to sing their hit song, "Butter."

BULLETPROOF BOYS

BTS stands for *Bangtan Sonyeondan*. This means "Bulletproof Boy Scouts" in English.

During a dance break, BTS plays air guitars. The boys move to center stage. Backup dancers join them. They end their song and strike a pose. The crowd cheers!

WHO IS BTS?

BTS is a **K-pop** band from South Korea. All seven members work together to make pop music. They also make rap and hip-hop music. They have won many music awards.

BTS

Members
J-Hope, Jimin, Jin, Jung Kook, RM, Suga, and V

Date Debuted
June 2013

Types of Music
pop, rap, hip-hop

First Hit
"No More Dream"

BTS SPEAKING OUT AGAINST RACISM

BTS supports **charities**. Members J-Hope, Jimin, and Suga have even given money to their hometowns. BTS also speaks out against **racism**.

BECOMING THE BOY BAND

The BTS members became interested in music in different ways. RM began rapping in middle school. V started playing the saxophone at a young age. Jimin, J-Hope, and Jung Kook attended a school to learn dance.

RM

DIY MUSICIANS

All of the BTS members write music for the group. RM alone has written over 200 songs for BTS!

Suga began to write his own music in high school. Jin wanted to be an actor at first but chose to be a singer instead.

Each BTS member joined the group at a different time. RM, Jimin, J-Hope, V, Jin, and Suga **auditioned** for what is now called BigHit Music.

RM, JIMIN, AND J-HOPE

FAVORITES

Show
J-Hope likes *Crash Landing On You*

Food
RM likes Korean knife-cut noodles

Artist
Jin likes Shawn Mendes

Drink
Jung Kook likes banana milk

Jung Kook showed his singing skills on a Korean TV show. Many companies wanted him, but he chose BigHit Music. The group was formed! They trained together before they **debuted**.

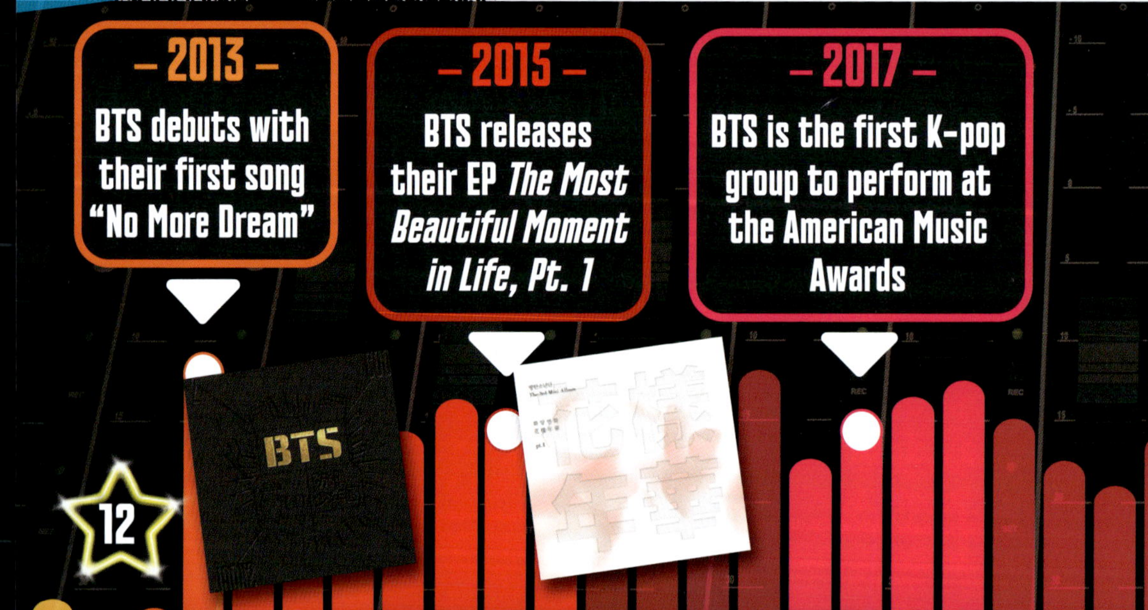
– 2013 –
BTS debuts with their first song "No More Dream"
– 2015 –
BTS releases their EP *The Most Beautiful Moment in Life, Pt. 1*
– 2017 –
BTS is the first K-pop group to perform at the American Music Awards
BTS

SKOOL LUV AFFAIR was one of their most popular **EPs**. It reached the ***Billboard*** World Albums chart. Later in 2014, BTS went on their first tour!

2020

BTS releases "Dynamite," their first song entirely in English

2021

BTS releases "Butter," their second song entirely in English

2022

BTS takes a break from music to join the South Korean military

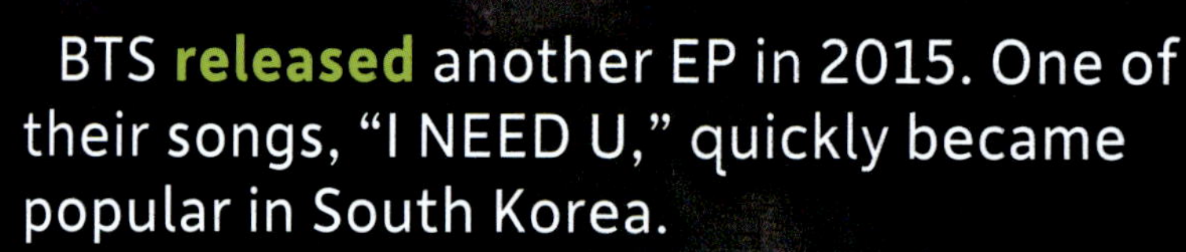

BTS **released** another EP in 2015. One of their songs, "I NEED U," quickly became popular in South Korea.

In 2016, BTS's album *The Most Beautiful Moment in Life: Young Forever* came out. New songs "Fire" and "Save ME" were hits! The album also includes popular songs from earlier albums like "DOPE" and "RUN."

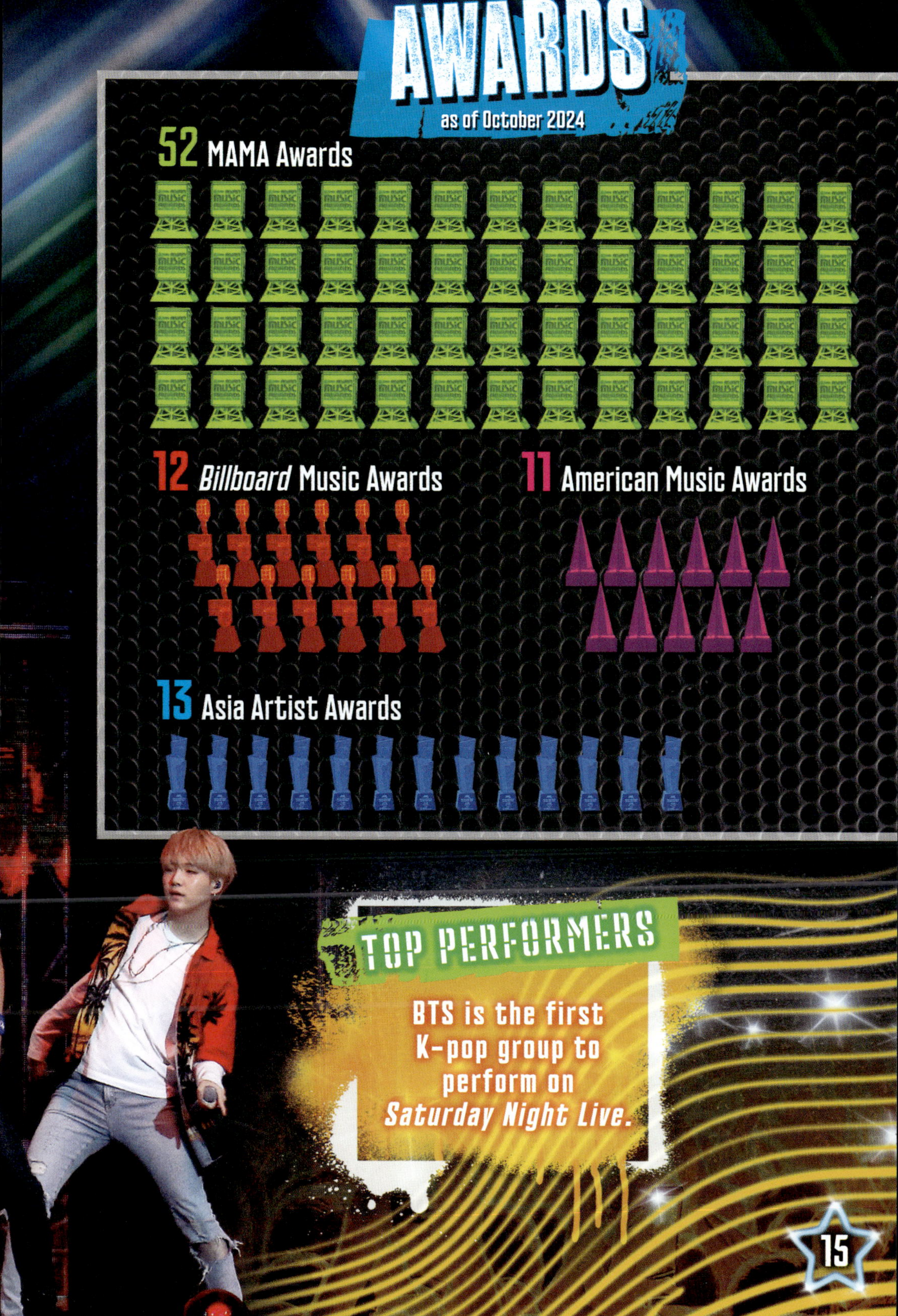

AWARDS

as of October 2024

52 MAMA Awards

12 *Billboard* Music Awards

11 American Music Awards

13 Asia Artist Awards

TOP PERFORMERS

BTS is the first K-pop group to perform on *Saturday Night Live*.

BTS had a big year in 2017. They were the first K-pop group **nominated** for a *Billboard* Music Award. They won and were named the Top Social Artist of the Year!

BTS also released their fifth EP. One of the songs, "DNA," made it to the *Billboard* Hot 100 chart. BTS started the Love Yourself world tour in 2018. It was a huge success!

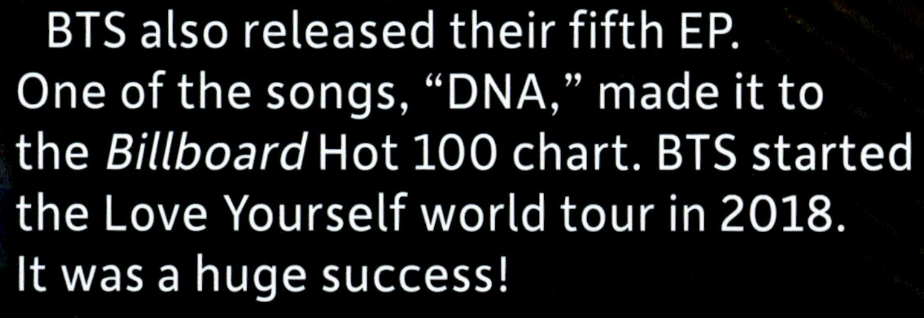

CUTE CHARACTERS

BTS has characters made after them. The members got to help make them. They are part of a line called BT21.

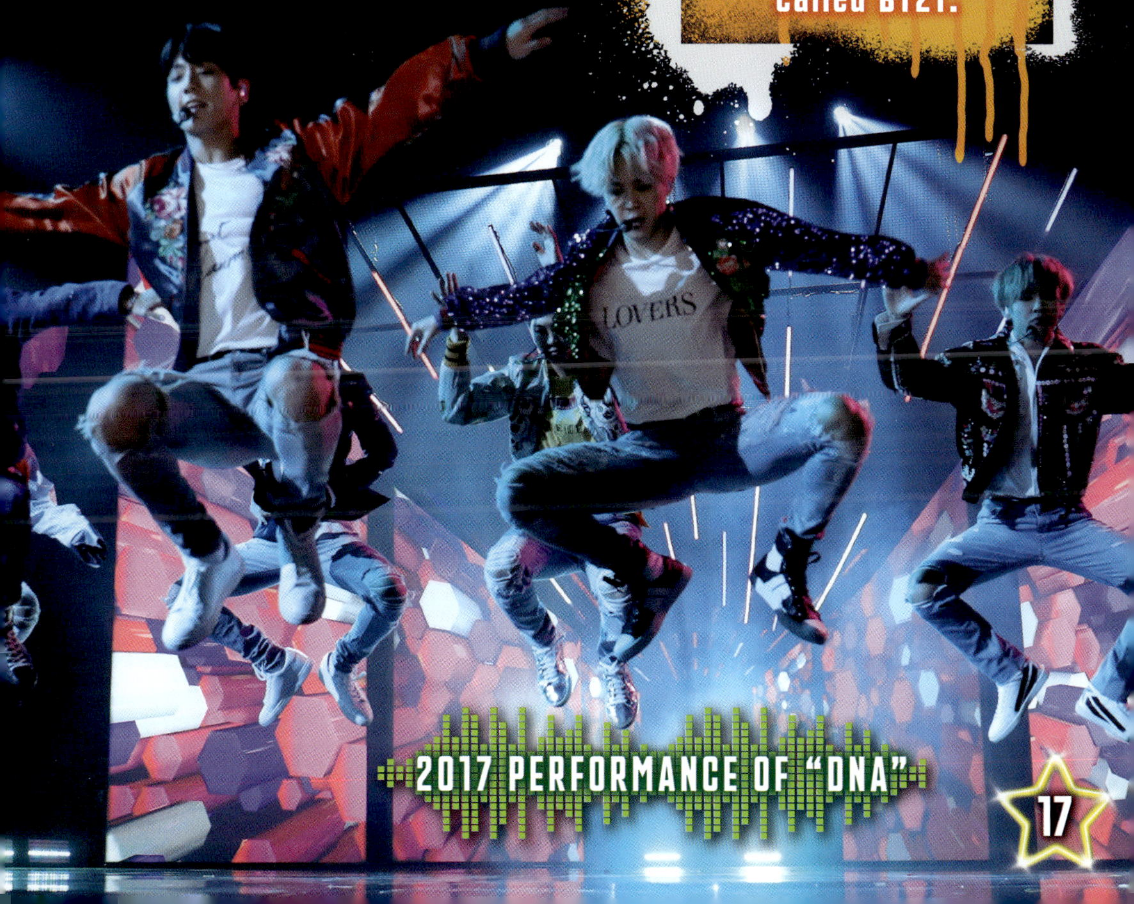

2017 PERFORMANCE OF "DNA"

BTS has worked with many artists. In 2019, they worked with pop artist Halsey. Together, they released a single called "Boy with Luv."

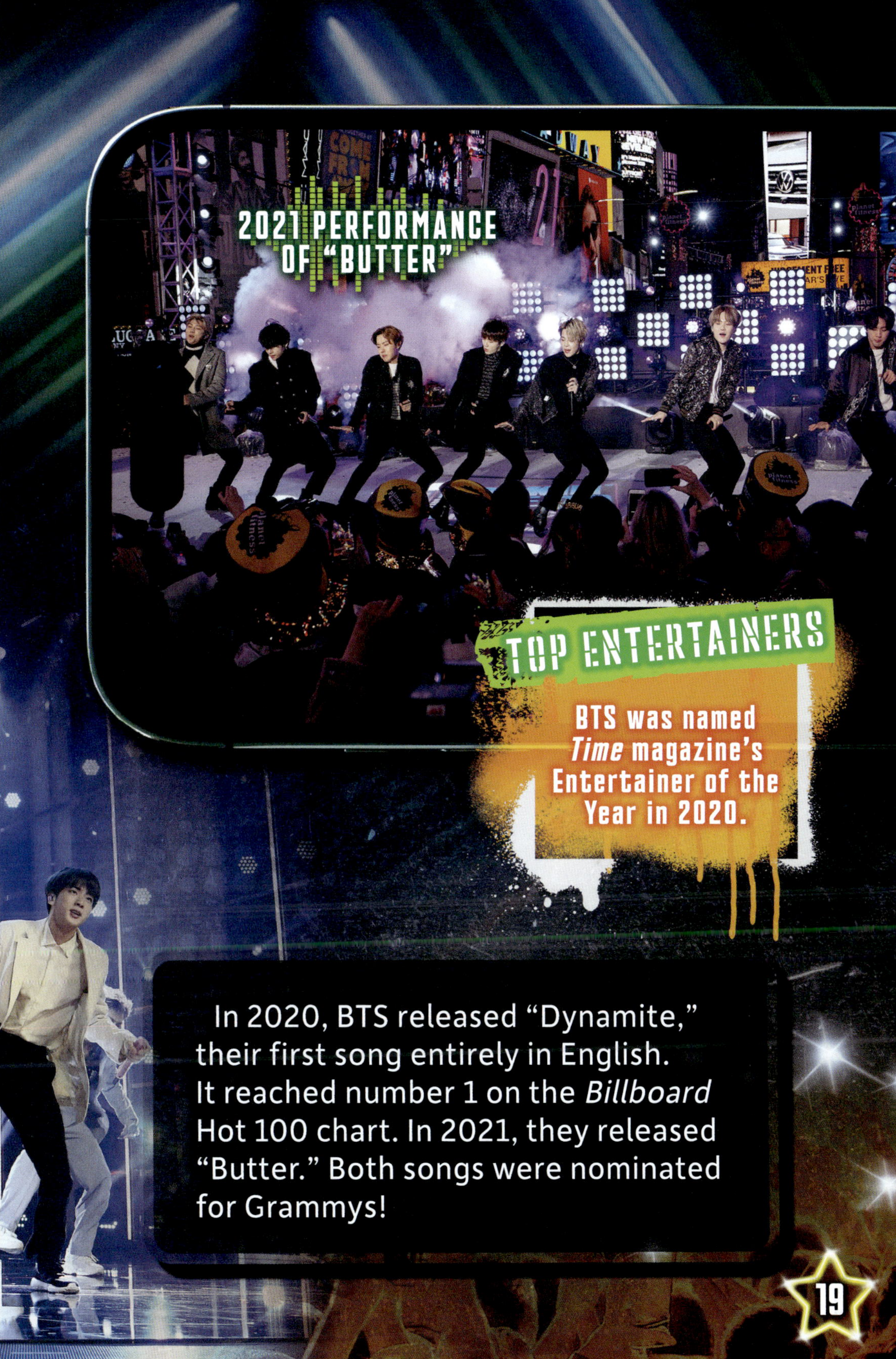

TOP ENTERTAINERS

BTS was named *Time* magazine's Entertainer of the Year in 2020.

In 2020, BTS released "Dynamite," their first song entirely in English. It reached number 1 on the *Billboard* Hot 100 chart. In 2021, they released "Butter." Both songs were nominated for Grammys!

FOR THE FANS

The BTS fan base is known as ARMY. It stands for Adorable Representative MC for Youth. Fans support BTS by **streaming** their music. ARMY members **chant** at concerts. They buy BTS **merchandise**!

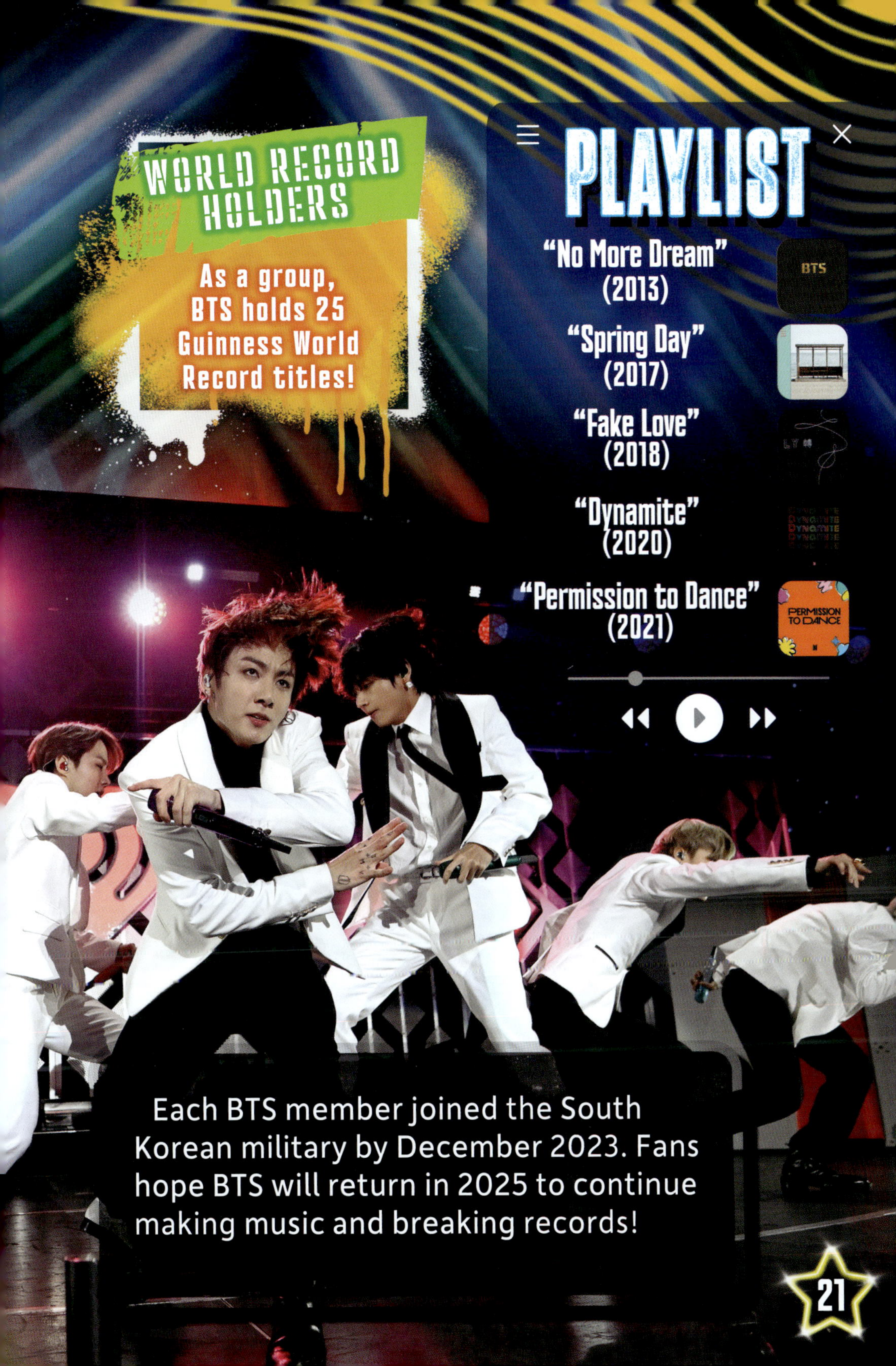

WORLD RECORD HOLDERS

As a group, BTS holds 25 Guinness World Record titles!

Each BTS member joined the South Korean military by December 2023. Fans hope BTS will return in 2025 to continue making music and breaking records!

GLOSSARY

auditioned—tried out for a role

Billboard—related to a well-known music news magazine and website that ranks songs and albums

chant—to repeat words, names, or phrases along with a group

charities—organizations that help others in need

debuted—was introduced or released for the first time

EPs—music recordings that are shorter than albums but have more songs than singles; EP stands for extended playlist.

Grammy Awards—yearly awards given by the Recording Academy of the United States for achievements in music; Grammy Awards are also called Grammys.

K-pop—related to pop music that comes from South Korea

merchandise—items a group or company makes to sell

nominated—chosen as a candidate for an award

racism—when people are treated unfairly because of their skin color or background

released—made music available for listening

streaming—playing music or other content from a service on the internet

TO LEARN MORE

AT THE LIBRARY

Holleran, Leslie. *BTS: K-Pop's Biggest Headliners.* Minneapolis, Minn.: Lerner Publications, 2024.

Loh-Hagan, Virginia. *The BTS ARMY.* Ann Arbor, Mich.: 45th Parallel Press, 2024.

Rustad, Martha E.H. *What You Never Knew About BTS.* North Mankato, Minn.: Capstone Press, 2022.

ON THE WEB

FACTSURFER

Factsurfer.com gives you a safe, fun way to find more information.

1. Go to www.factsurfer.com.
2. Enter "BTS" into the search box and click 🔍.
3. Select your book cover to see a list of related content.

INDEX

The images in this book are reproduced through the courtesy of: Efren Landaos/ Newscom, front cover (BTS); Catsense, front cover (background light); Taya Ovod, pp. 2-3; ZUMA Press/ Alamy, p. 3; Kevin Mazur/ Getty Images, pp. 4, 18-19, 21; Chris Pizzello/ Invision/ AP Newsroom, pp. 4-5; Jordan Strauss/ Invision/ AP Newsroom, p. 6; Kevin Dietsch/ Getty Images, p. 7; ABACAPRESS/ Alamy, pp. 7 (infographic), 11 (Shawn Mendes); Scott Roth/ Invision/ AP Newsroom, p. 8; WENN Rights Ltd/ Alamy, p. 9; JTBC PLUS/ Imazins/ Getty Images, p. 10; Bulletproof7BTS/ Wikipedia, pp. 11, 12-13; Busyblue4/ Wikipedia, p. 11 (*Crash Landing On You*); CHALLA_81, p. 11 (noodles); Sky1wave, p. 11 (banana milk); Dabarti CGI, pp. 12-13 (timeline mixing board); jbrink, pp. 12-13, 21 (playlist); Paul Zimmerman/ Getty Images, pp. 14-15; AFP/ Stringer/ Getty Images, p. 15 (MAMA Awards); Kathy Hutchins, p. 15 (*Billboard* Music Awards); s_bukley, p. 15 (American Music Awards); Selfiepod/ Wikipedia, p. 15 (Asia Artist Awards); THE FACT/ Imazins/ Getty Images, p. 16; Chris Polk/ AMA2017/ Getty Images, pp. 16-17; zz/ John Nacion/ STAR MAX/ IPx/ AP Newsroom, p. 19; Debra L Rothenberg/ FilmMagic/ Getty Images, p. 20; Xavier Collin/ Image Press Agency/ Sipa USA/ Alamy, p. 23.